SHTUM
The Stutter Poems

David Bateman

IRON PRESS

First published 2016 by IRON Press
5 Marden Terrace
Cullercoats
North Shields
NE30 4PD
tel/fax +44(0)191 2531901
ironpress@blueyonder.co.uk
www.ironpress.co.uk

FIRST EDITION

ISBN 978-0-9931245-4-9
Printed by Ingram Lightning Source

Poems © David Bateman 2016
This collection copyright IRON Press 2016
All David Bateman photos by Philip Gorry
Cover and Book Design Brian Grogan

Typeset in Georgia
IRON Press books are distributed by NBN International
and represented by Inpress Ltd
Churchill House, 12 Mosley Street,
Newcastle upon Tyne, NE1 1DE
tel: +44(0)191 2308104
www.inpressbooks.co.uk

David Bateman hereby asserts his right
under the Copyright, Designs and Patents Act 1988
to be identified as the author of this work.

Supported using public funding by
ARTS COUNCIL ENGLAND
LOTTERY FUNDED

David Bateman

ORIGINALLY FROM RIVER HILL IN RURAL WEST KENT, DAVID BATEMAN arrived in Liverpool via Middlesbrough and Leasowe. Having had a severe stutter as a child and teenager, he finally had successful speech therapy in Liverpool in 1980, and though still stuttering slightly in ordinary life, has since performed his poetry widely, winning numerous poetry slams and competitions. He has also read poetry on local and national BBC radio, and was a winner on Dave Gorman's comedy TV show, *Genius,* with his scheme to make the Isle Of Wight symmetrical.

As well as poetry, he writes stories and occasional scripts and articles; he has worked as a writer and facilitator for various arts projects, and also as a creative writing tutor, including much work in mental health resource centres. Recently he has worked with the Canning History Project, set in the Canning Street area of Liverpool, and is working with composer Tommy Moss on a musical comedy for stage, *Spooks! – Things That Go Bump.*

His poetry publications include *Curse Of The Killer Hedge* (IRON Press 1996), *A Homage To Me* (Driftwood 2003), and *More Spit Than Polish, Volume 1: Scorpion Farm* (Reprobate 2012). He also edited the Liverpool anthology, *The Dead Good Poets Society: The Book* (Headland 2005), and his poetry for children has appeared in over 20 anthologies.

Acknowledgements

Some of these poems and prose pieces (or earlier versions of them) have been previously published in the magazines *Citizen 32, In The Red, New Horizon, Nightingale* and *the-phone-book.com;* in the anthologies *Waiting: winning entries in the Sefton Writing Competition* (Driftwood 2007) and *Climb Every Mountain (Or Not): poems and stories, 2006–2008,* by the South Drive Creative Writing Group (Reprobate 2008); and on the anthology cassette, *Suburban Relapse,* compiled by John A (Chuck) Connor (Skate Press, 1982). My thanks to the various editors.

The poem 'The Utter Glamour' is shamelessly recycled from my booklet, *The Utter Glamour* (Reprobate 2009).

Several of the poems were first broadcast on BBC Radio Merseyside, mostly on the *First Friday* strand of the *Roger Phillips* show. Cheers to Roger and to Sylvia Hikins.

Special thanks to Gary Hastie, who approached me in May 2009 to take part in a BBC Radio Merseyside documentary about stuttering. It was this that prompted me to re-read my earlier diary and poetry on stuttering and speech therapy, which in turn inspired an outpouring of new poetry. 'Shtum' and an excerpt from 'The Utter Glamour' were broadcast in Gary's documentary (produced by Pauline McAdam and himself), *The Queen's English,* on BBC Radio Merseyside in 2011.

Thanks to Mike Cunningham for the time, wisdom and tact he put into critically commenting on the collection in its early stages. Thanks also to Vik, Lawrence Pettener, Alan Humphrey and Penelope Hope for their comments and help. Thanks to the fantastically hard-working Pete Mortimer of Iron Press for many things, including his patience during the odd stutter in preparing this book.

Many of these poems have been performed here and there around Britain's poetry venues. Cheers to the organizers and audiences, and especially to the Dead Good Poets Society in Liverpool.

To those who stammer
and those who stutter
I dedicate
these reams of splutter.

CONTENTS

	Page
Shtum	11
Goodbye To All The Patter	14
שטוטש סוטש (Welcome To The Word Void)	14
Not The Ones Who'll Last	15
Is This Your Own Work?	16
The Mapping Of Causes By Family Doctor (Our Stutterer A Tender 7 Years Old)	17
The Same Boy	18
The Origami Of Rubbish On The Wind	19
What You Could Get For Tenpence	20
My Official Timed Record For Longest Single-Word Stutter	20
Ho Ho Ho (And A Monster Is Born)	22
The Invisible Monkey	23
Always And Sometimes	24
Shtum Static	25
The Native Eloquence	26
Barbarians	27
At Night	28
The Most Reliable Way To Speak No Evil	29
The Mapping Of Causes By Conversations With Other People (Our Stutterer A Tender 16 Years Old)	30
Rare Example Of Successful Joke During Conversations About My Stutter	31
The Critical Commentary	31
In The Sweetshop	32
It's Hard To Be Suave With A Stutter	33
Posh Love Poem	35
Stammer Or Stutter?	36
The Run-Up	36
Talking So Fast	37
On Having A Stutter	38
Dream	39

Against Words	40
Me And My Stutter	41
The Stutter The Symbol	42
The Masker	43
Syllabic Speech	43
Less To Me Than Meets The Eye	44
A Top PR Man From West Kirby...	45
Trouble With Your Nerves	46
Fog	47
Bastard Bloody Stutter	48
A Cup Of Tea In Stormsville	49
The Good News, The Bad News, & The Therapeutic Chorus	50
The Life And Soul	51
Two Hours To Go	51
Jonah	53
Twitch	54
Intensive Speech Therapy Course, Day 9	55
The 'Before' Film	56
Another 'Before' Film	57
Five Minutes / It Was Never Like This	58
Coming Down	60
Avoidance Tactics	61
Why I Hate Doing Street Assignments With Other People From The Group	62
Just One Sonetto (Sonetto Faceto)	63
The Utter Glamour	64
The Stutter Rides Off Into The Sunset (Unfortunately At Roughly The Same Speed As Myself)	67
In Praise Of The Human Voice	68
British Stammering Association	70

Shtum

S h t u m

1

Words are untrustworthy
cantankerous contraptions,
my life story a silent film
with poetry as the captions.

2

Something gruesome has occurred
to each once well-meaning word.
Its start has come apart,
and its ending can't be heard.

It's perfidious, insidious,
invidious and hideous.
In the matter of chatter,
you start to be fastidious.

3

I've got this stutter.
Tend to squawk when I mutter.
My words cut like a blade
of grass through frozen butter.

I stick and I splutter
on every sentence I utter.
The spoken word's an open world
beyond a locked-up shutter.

4

It's a world of Never mind,
It doesn't matter,
and Forget it.
It's a world that turns
away again,
before you've even met it.

5

Every day taking obsessive care
to have just the right fare
for the bus when I pay it.
Laying out the right amount
for the driver to count,
in case I can't say it.

6

Now that talking's a crime
with no chance of repentance,
you're serving your time,
every sentence a sentence.

7

Behind what behind what
What behind what
Behind what behind what
What behind what
Behind what I'm saying
Behind what I'm not
Behind what I'm stuck on
Behind what I've got
Behind what my face is
Behind how it twists
Behind what's now showing
Behind what exists
Behind what's beyond me
Behind what's not mine
Behind what's my body
Behind what's no sign
Behind what I'm saying
Behind what I'm not
Behind what I'm stuck on
Behind what I've got
Behind what behind what
What behind what
Behind what behind what
What behind what

Goodbye To All The Patter

Say goodbye to all the patter
as your throat becomes a clam:
any further subject matter
can remain behind its dam –

and your syllables will shatter
from plain sense to cryptogram,
as the tripping spastic clatter
crumbles truth into a sham.

Best abandon any plan
you might've had including chatter,
wave farewell, and, if you can,
say goodbye to all the patter.

שוטש שטום
(Welcome To The Word Void)

Welcome to the word void
where the fear of the slip
brings silence; welcome and
שטום now, hush your lip.

Welcome to the age-old
comfortable silence, the role
of the good listener, the world
where you shut your hole.

Welcome to the word void
as if it is some strange Elysium
of peace; here is only one word
and the word is שטום.

Not The Ones Who'll Last

We're your friends and you can trust us.
You can be with us and play.

These are your friends:
John, Peter, Mike and Paul.
These are your friends,
and here in the playground
you don't know what they're doing
till they've got you surrounded.

With your stutter
we will mock you,
shut you out and
lock the door.
Expect you'll get
upset now, won't you?
When you do,
we'll mock you more.

You get up off the ground
so they can knock you down again.
Sometimes your life, like your voice,
stutters.
Things don't turn out how you meant them to
or sometimes don't turn out at all.
Sentences turn into silence.
Friends turn into enemies.

Buh-Buh-Bateman,
Buh-Buh-Bateman,
we'll play chase,
and you are It.
You cuh-cuh-can't
catch us, can you?
Cos you're a
puh-piece of –

We're your friends and you can trust us.
You've no others anyway.

You get up off the ground
so they can knock you down again.
You get up off the ground
so they can knock you down again.

Is This Your Own Work?

The moving hands of the staff room clock
creep towards the first lesson of the afternoon,
while beneath it, the more literal moving hand
of Guy Pearce marks each of the pile
of First Year Geography essays,
and having marked, moves on to the next:
the usual mix of the halfway decent,
the bad, and the illegible.
Eight out of ten, five out of ten,
four out of ten.
Near the end of the pile,
a short but implausibly fluent essay
from the stuttering idiot in the third row
who's never once answered a single question
in two months of classes.
Question mark out of ten.
Is this your own work?

The Mapping Of Causes By Family Doctor
(Our Stutterer A Tender 7 Years Old)

Are you often nervous?
Are you ever nervous at school?
Do you worry much?
Does school ever worry you?
Do you have nightmares very often?

These sudden strange questions
make me nervous from the start.
Without even knowing I am lying,
I play safe, and answer
Nernernernerno to all of them.

The Same Boy

THE SAME BOY IS IN EVERY PRIMARY SCHOOL I GO TO, AND HE'S always stuck. I bomb round from school to school with my specialist workshops and I've half-forgotten them the moment I've finished my report: a daze of trains, taxis, staffrooms, classrooms of children with eager hands raised, children settling down to the enjoyably challenging exercises I've set; but as I walk round the class, I find the same boy is there again, and he's still stuck.

He's a small boy: trimmed black hedgehog haircut, nervous mouth, evasive eyes, and he can't even articulate what the problem is.

Discovering him, I sensed a chance to reach back into my own desperate past to change things, and tried ever harder to get through, to help; but somehow I'm still never doing quite the right thing, and what's almost worse, I feel I never will; and there we both are, stuck.

The Origami Of Rubbish On The Wind

At the bus stop
a man is showing his four-year-old son
the origami of rubbish on the wind.
A cartwheeling binbag is two dogs fighting.
A scuttling strip of corrugated cardboard:
a cat crossing the road.
It is a fleeting art,
mostly gone by the time
the son has chance to look.
But even he sees the wind-whipped newspaper
now suddenly a pigeon taking flight.
A wave of crisp packets along the pavement
is a herd of stampeding guinea pigs;
and while waiting for my bus I wait also
for swans, penguins, elephants, vultures,
frogs, turtles, unicorns, pteranodons.
A commotion of fluttering above us
and this time the son is first,
pointing upwards and shouting Look! Look!
No, says his father: Those are real pigeons.
They don't count.

What You Could Get For Tenpence

FOR A WHILE, THE BUS FARE TO SCHOOL WAS EXACTLY TENPENCE. IT seems such a tiny amount now. I'd put down the change I'd got ready beforehand. One fivepence, two twos and one one. This way the driver would know I didn't want a ninepence or an eightpence, if such things existed; and let's face it: I wasn't going to ask.

It's bad enough getting stuck in the middle of saying something long. But getting stuck on just saying your bus fare, with everybody on the bus waiting and watching you screw up your face as you try to say it: that's almost the worst.

And what for? School was the last place I wanted to go, because the moment we arrived and the lads on the bus met up with their mates outside the school, it was going to be pain all the way, and even when I got away from those, it was going to be just the same lot but with different faces in my own class; the same on and off for the whole day, because having a stutter at school was like having a special sign saying VICTIM, even to the teachers, and even to my so-called friends.

It was amazing what you could get for tenpence in those days.

My Official Timed Record For Longest Single-Word Stutter

I WAS ROUND AT GEOFF'S PLACE, AND WE WERE IN HIS LIVING ROOM, listening to his records. Let's say that we were listening to side one of *Tarkus* by Emerson, Lake & Palmer. This becomes important later. I was fourteen and he'd turned fifteen. Geoff's place was a maisonette above Tesco's in Sevenoaks High Street, where he and his mum and sister lived. It was easy to tell the time there, because there was a clock with a two-foot wide face sticking out from the wall just outside the window.

Geoff could sometimes be a bit of a bastard to me when we were with other friends, doing things like taking my stuff and cycling off with it, but he was nearly always alright when it was just the two of us. So we were listening to music at his, and talking, and naturally I was stuttering like always.

Anyway, there was a certain moment, and a certain track on the album was just finishing, and I was trying to say something, I can't remember what now, but I got stuck on it, and it just would not come out. The tune that was finishing finished, and the next one started, and I was still trying to say whatever it was I was trying to say, and I still wasn't getting a single word out. Nothing unusual so far: I'd often get stuck for half a minute, or even a whole one, on one word, but this block just carried on and on. Geoff took a guess at what I was going to say, and I shook my head and kept on trying to get the first word out. And I kept on trying and failing, and the music was carrying on in the background, and I was still stuck, and then that tune finished and the next one started, and I was *still* stuck, and Geoff was still waiting, and then eventually, finally, after this stupidly long time, I finally said whatever it was I was trying to say, and then the conversation carried on, and my stutters in it from there on were all of a more modest sort.

Anyway, the point is that afterwards, when I got home, I went into the dining room where the record player was, and pulled out my own copy of *Tarkus,* and played the bit that I'd got stuck during, and timed it.

It was something over three minutes.

In the years since then, I've probably done a few other stutters that rival that one, but thankfully not too many, and none of them recent, so I always remember that particular stutter as my PW or personal worst, and as my official timed record for longest single-word stutter.

Ho Ho Ho (And A Monster Is Born)

Several times now, I've heard stand-up comedians on TV and radio saying how they were bullied for a little while at school, but found they could get out of it by coming out with jokes and with fast, funny answers to the other kids. How easy they make speaking sound!

Imagine the scene: it's a lovely sunny playground where unfortunately I am in the grip of two playmates, one on each of my ears. Fortunately however, I have just thought up a very funny joke. Unfortunately because of my stutter, I can't get a bloody word out and I'm still just stuck with this very funny joke in my head and a so-called schoolmate still holding each of my ears.

Oh, how they would let go of my ears and roll around with hysterical laughter if only I could actually deliver this very funny joke that I've just miraculously thought up! How they would slap me gently and apologetically on the back as they welcome me into their club of people who are never bullied, who are at worst just slightly joshed! How they would henceforth wait on my every witty word, the gems I will bring out with such elegance, such timing, such pants-wetting funniness.

Yes, I think to myself, I'll make them piss their pants, the bastards. *I'll* take the piss out of *them* for a change.

The Invisible Monkey

I WASN'T BORN WITH A STUTTER: THERE WAS A TIME WHEN I WAS small when I could talk without stuttering, so it's not like the stutter was always there, just waiting for me to start talking so I could start stuttering at the same time. The stutter was something I got later, after a year or so of school; but after a year of stuttering my way through primary school it already seemed like something that might as well have always been there with me. From the playground to the sweetshop, from the classroom to the girl you think of asking out but never do of course, the stutter's there with you every minute of your talking life. It's like that invisible monkey in that old ghost story about the haunted priest on the green tea, the doomed priest with the invisible monkey gradually taking over more & more of his life. All that the other schoolkids see is the way you cower from this beast that they can't even see. You screw up your face quite a bit when you try to talk – you don't want to, you just want to talk, but what they see is the grimaces which don't mean anything, grimaces which look like expressions of god knows what, look like the monkey's expressions, but only you know what the monkey really looks like, monkey with its claws in your throat, – then again if your expressions look like the monkey's, maybe in a way they really do see it, do see the monkey, but they think it's you, think that's what you are, – & that's why you always get cut out of everything, – they don't want to see that monkey, that's why they tend to avoid looking at you, why they're all talking over whatever you're trying to say, & again & again until finally you just give up, – because the monkey is what they see now & you yourself long ago became invisible.

Always And Sometimes

I always had the words in my head.
I could just never say them.
My thoughts are all lined up to be said
But my throat won't obey them.

And everyone thinks
It's a pretty good joke
That a mouthful of words
Seems to make me choke

– They say that I talk
Like a dud machine-gun:
Rapid fire, twenty words,
And they're all the same one;

And I wish that they were made out of lead
Sometimes when I spray them.

Shtum Static

stammer dammed
gored grammar
dumb mummer
mouth clammer
stood stupid
lip slabber
stuck stubborn
jibber jabber
shtum static
throat clatter
tongue monkey
tough matter
mutter numbed
nothing but the
stutter
stutter
stutter
stutter

The Native Eloquence

There's a faithful realism at least, like O'Neill says:
stammering is the native eloquence of us fog people.
Stammering can be a tool that is all the more powerful for
    not being a tool,
but how can I use it?
As a demonstration of itself.
As a manifestation of my own apartness.
As a caricature of all communication.
& to say Fuck you if you don't care.
A STAMMER ISN'T EXACTLY WHAT YOU'D CALL
    VERSATILE.
It is a bearer of limited images.
It is a rough-poetic device I can't switch off.

Barbarians

Greek βάρβαρος, barbaros: foreign, uncultured, ignorant.
Sanskrit बर्बर, barbara: stuttering, gibbering, foreign, fool.

It comes down from the ancients,
Whether Indian or Greek:
A handy name to call the fools
Who don't know how to speak.

The gibberish of foreigners
Is all just 'bar-bar-bar' –
The clattering of stammerers,
Of those with no savoir.

The stutterer, the idiot,
Or anyone non-Aryan,
With every bleat or bray betrays
Himself as a barbarian.

Our tangled mangled language
Gives offence to god and man.
We've got them scoffing and a-scolding:
Bar-bar-bar-barbarian!

So forgive us now our dumbnesses,
We beg, O mighty Jingo!
Forgive us – we barbarians
Who can't quite speak the lingo.

At Night

At night, when I've done my homework, I write. Anything.
   Poems, dreams, whatever's happened. Anything.
If they come in, I cover it up with homework as if I'm still
   working on that, but when they've gone to bed I can
   write as much as I like. Myths, new worlds, anything.
Each night like a small miracle, the words appearing on the
   page are the words I meant to say, not like the cheap and
   broken imitations I'm forced to speak each day.
Exercise books can be trusted: you can talk to them like you
   can't talk to people.
You can talk to friends sometimes, but the words get broken
   up, broken apart: nothing ever comes out quite how it's
   meant to.
You're better off with writing; you're better off at night.

The Most Reliable Way To Speak No Evil

Interesting things come out boring.
I learnt to be concise.
Jokes come out unfunny.
I learnt not to mess with them.
A comment on the weather might last a lifetime.
I don't have small talk at all.

Saying the wrong & mundane things
& getting them wrong:
that's not such a disappointing failure.
But then anything right or beautiful
just comes out ugly too...

The most reliable way to speak no evil
is to keep your mouth shut.

The Mapping Of Causes
By Conversations With Other People
(Our Stutterer A Tender 16 Years Old)

THIS IS DIFFICULT, TRYING TO GET A LOT OF CONVERSATIONS ALL into one. So what we'll do is imagine a composite friend of a friend for me to talk with. I will play me aged 16, and you will play the composite friend of a friend, which is an excellent part, because it means you don't have a stutter. On the other hand, it also means responsibility, and that it will be your fault if this goes wrong. So, let's say we've just met now, and I've just stuttered really badly with you for the first time. Here we go.

– Excuse my stutter.
– That's okay. Do you usually stutter?
– Yes: it's usually even worse than this.
– Have you stuttered long?
– Since I was about 6.
– Are you a nervous person?
– No, I don't really think so.
– Not at all?
– Well sometimes I get nervous about my stutter ha ha.
– Does that affect you? I mean do you sometimes not say things when you want to?
– No.
– Do you mind me asking you questions about your stutter?
– No. It's one of my favourite subjects actually.
– Does anyone else in your family stutter?
– My dad did when he was young. He sometimes stutters very slightly now when he's got a lot to say or when he's had a bit to drink.
– Ah, so it might be hereditary then?
– It might be.
– You said you usually stutter more than now. Does it vary a lot?
– Yeah.
– Do you find it changes with your mood, or with different people?
– No, I don't.
– Oh.

What sensible nonsense I talked back then! How stolidly
my surface-self surrendered all ambition! How little I gave
and gave away! How quick it's always your turn to talk once
again! (And by the way, I thought you played your part quite
well, considering.)

Rare Example Of Successful Joke During Conversations About My Stutter

Have you stuttered long?
Sussometimes up to 3 minutes ha ha.

The Critical Commentary

How I wish he could get it all out a bit faster:
It's all very fine having something to say,
But I wish that whatever he's saying was shorter,
And I wish he'd not screw up his face in that way.

He pulls all those faces: it makes you feel awkward.
If he'd just breathe in deeply, I'm sure it would stop,
But he just carries on with those silent contortions:
It's a wonder he ever gets served in a shop.

In The Sweetshop

Thank you, madam... Yes sir?
Uh –
Yes, sir?
Uh – Uh – Uh –
You're not going to be sick, are you?
Uh – Uh –
Could you go outside if you're going to be sick. Not on the
    counter.
Uh – Uh –
Could you go outside:
I do not want sick on my counter.
I do not want sick on my Kit-Kats
        my Polos
        my Bounties
        my Mars Bars
I do not want sick on my Cadbury's Flakes
        my Amazin' Raisin Bars.

It's Hard To Be Suave With A Stutter

I dream of being eloquent with upper-crusted tones,
My repartee so elegant and bright.
Sophisticated soirées will become my rightful home,
My words just like a charm of birds in flight.

But it's hard to be suave with a stutter:
It's hard to be a breezy sort of bloke.
If, when you order champers,
You get stuck on 'sha–,' it hampers
You in mingling smoothly with the gentler folk.

I'd be the life and soul of every dinner party thrown:
My company would be most keenly sought;
My every witty story would be keenly hung upon,
From first aperitifs through to the port.

But it's hard to be suave with a stutter:
It's hard to be a chatty sort of chap.
When you're telling jokes but tending
To get stuck before the ending,
It tends to take out something of the snap.

Oh, bad enough to have a dad whose job is mending cars,
And a mum who works at cleaning all day long;
Oh, bad enough to find I'm born outside the upper class,
But to have a stutter too – Well, that's just wrong.

For it's hard to be suave with a stutter:
It's hard to be a dashing sort of dude.
All the spitting and the snorting
At the débutante you're courting
Can tend to dampen something of the mood.

I dream of being slick and glib with stardust on my tongue:
The grandest MC yet to grace the room,
With streams of words that scintillate like fireflies in the dusk,
A subtle bouquet bursting into bloom.

But it's hard to be suave with a stutter:
It's hard to be a jaunty sort of gent.
When your very best oration
Has no words, just punctuation,
It can slightly sap the zest from the event.

Posh Love Poem

I love you awfully.
I love you terribly.
I love you horribly.

How grotesquely I love you!
How disgustingly I love you!
How appalling is my love
And how quite gruesome!

How abominably, abhorrently
and loathsomely I love you!
With what unpleasantness,
offensiveness and vileness!

I love you hideously.
I love you frightfully.
I love you awfully.

Stammer Or Stutter?

Is it 'stammer'? Is it 'stutter'?
Just which one should you utter?
Or might your choice upset me,
by the bye?

Well, I think you're free to use
whichever word you choose,
and when my voice will let me,
so am I.

The Run-Up

yes and you know like
for say a high-jumper
to have a good run-up
is part of his art

yes and you know like
to talk if you stutter
you too feel you need one
to give you a start

Talking So Fast

I'm talking so fast
now at last I've begun
I'm talking so fast
to get it over and done

I'm talking so fast
to get the simple words through
I'm talking so fast
because that's what I do

I've been silent so long, and that silence is slow
when I'm still there in the starting-block long after the go
I've been itching and twitching, not giving you a hint
Now I've started at last, I'll fit it all in one sprint

I'm talking so fast
in these spurts of my voice
I'm talking so fast
while I've got any choice

I'm talking so fast
because I can't risk a pause
I'm talking so fast
to escape from the claws

I've been silent so long, and that silence is stiff
when the time to talk is not a case of when but of if
I've been waiting impatient, behind a hard block
and now the words are flying, flying out in a flock

I'm talking so fast
and the words rush and seethe
I'm talking so fast
and I can't stop to breathe

I'm talking so fast
while I've got a clear track
I'm talking so fast
before the block comes back

I'm talking so fast
in case I stop, and what then?
I'm talking so fast
in case I can't start again

I'm talking so fast
now at last I've begun
I'm talking so fast
to get it over and done

On Having A Stutter

To err is human
and to um is fine,
but having a stutter
is a bit of a swine.

D r e a m

on a chair
in a room
in the light
in the dark

in the mist
in the warmth
a sleeper
a truant

tonight
on my own
in the music
the quiet

my stutterized soul

is silent
is fluent

Against Words

Dribbling out of mouths and pencils,
Pens and printers, speakers, stencils,
Words are rampant, words are rife,
Words will tangle up your life.

They never say just what you mean.
Turquoise always comes out green.
Double-meanings change the hue
So lily-white can come out blue.

Words are bastards.
Words are turds.
Words are bitches.
I hate words.

Changing slightly every day,
Not meaning what you meant to say.
There's words for that: 'semantic drift'
When meanings slyly slip and shift.

Words are so much useless clutter.
Words are cruel to those who stutter.
Word-games fill your mind with babble.
Burn the crossword! Bin the Scrabble!

Words are buggers.
Words are gits.
Words are just a
Bunch of shits.

Words corrupt, cos words are power,
Words will turn your whole life sour.
Words defy their definitions.
Leave them to the politicians.

Words onscreen will clog your disk.
Don't let them stay. Don't take the risk.
Don't let them reach the printout sheet.
Just block them in, then press DELETE.

Words are bastards.
Words are turds.
Words are bitches.
I hate words.

Me And My Stutter

Me and my stut—ter
Listening to the singer sing
Me and my stut—ter
Seeing what the night might bring

And though it might seem tough
We don't really care –
For us it seems enough
Just that the music's there

And me and my stut—ter
Never need to say a thing

The Stutter The Symbol

the stutter
the symbol
the symbol of my stutter
not a symbol of me
except the symbol of me stuttering
the symbol of itself
the gobbler-up of words
the swallower-down and the spitter-out
of the words I was going to use
the little monster on the wind
the swift voracious word-eater
the snatcher and the spoiler
the pillager and parasite
the symbol not of me
but the symbol of itself
the symbol of my stutter
the symbol
the stutter

The Masker

You fix the strap neatly round your neck,
make sure the little flat mike
is right against your Adam's apple,
shove the phones in your ears,
hit the switch on the box and –

(always assuming you can get that difficult first syllable out)

speak

and WHSSSSHHHH!!!!!!!!
a blast of white noise in your ears
and you're away.
'Listen! Listen everybody, I can talk!
I'm not stuttering! I'm normal!'
'Yes, and that's a very fetching
choker you're wearing today, Dave.'

Syllabic Speech

Think tick tock tick tock.
Say tick tock tick tock.
Good. Now talk like it.

I want to rush out and say:
Liss sen ev ry bod dy
I can talk I'm not stut
ter ring now I'm nor mal!

but I know they will only
say something like:
Normal on Skaro maybe, Dave,
but not in Middlesbrough.

Less To Me Than Meets The Eye

My eye is clear, my voice is smooth:
Decisive tones that lull and soothe,
Ideal for meeting someone new.
I'm pleased to meet you. How d'you do?
My skin is clean, untouched by germ,
My chin is strong, my handshake firm,
My manner, clothes and mind are smart;
My conversation – like an art;
But still you'll guess, as time goes by,
There's less to me than meets the eye.

My bosses love the way I work
And seize upon my useful quirk
For meeting strangers, closing deals,
Smoothing feathers, oiling wheels;
They urge me on to give my most;
Then move me round from post to post.
Promotions come; but all the same,
They'll soon enough forget my name.
It makes no odds how hard I try.
There's less to me than meets the eye.

At social functions, parties, sprees,
You can't help but be at your ease.
We loved tonight so very much.
We really ought to stay in touch.
Who knows? Perhaps you will at first,
But soon you'll find I've quenched that thirst.
Your first impressions are the best.
Beyond that, I'll fail every test.
Those who know me won't deny
There's less to me than meets the eye.

An easy word, a winning smile,
Can carry you a long, long while.
A job well done. A pleasant chat.
Success – there's none can argue that.
But still I wish I could ignore
Those hints I should be something more;
And as I play the perfect host,
Yet drift through life more like a ghost,
Sometimes I *almost* wonder why
There's less to me than meets the eye.

A Top PR Man From West Kirby...

A top PR man from West Kirby
Spoke in diction so perfectly blurby,
    It was all adjectival,
      With not one survival
Of anything nouny or verby.

Trouble With Your Nerves

Your next-door neighbour
says he can tell
that you've probably been having
a rough time recently.
He says this just after
you have stuttered quite a bit.
He may or may not have noticed
that you used to be half of a couple
and that now you are alone.
Swallows flit over the front garden
where you and he talk.
He says he can tell
that you have trouble with your nerves.
He used to have trouble with his nerves too,
he says. It was some years back,
he was working too hard,
and he let things get on top of him
and had to go into hospital:
you know, a breakdown.
He says you were too soft on that kid
you caught the other day,
from the gang that broke the windows.
He says you have to learn to be harder
like him, or like your landlord,
with whom he is good friends.
Your neighbour and you both look again
for a few seconds at the broken windows.
He says that if they'd done that to him,
he'd have set the dogs on them,
and that if they'd tried anything on him,
he'd have paralysed them,
and that three fingers is all it takes.
He says he used to be in the SD
and that he can paralyse or kill anyone.
He says that one night
he caught four men buggering around
breaking things in his garden,
and that the SD always go for
the eyes and the throat

and he soon had them tied up
just over there. He says that he can
be either a good friend or
a very bad enemy and that he has
a kind heart underneath.

F o g

You and your stutter
have somehow become
not only less audible
but less visible too,
and now again you welcome it:
the fog that rolls in across the sea wall,
rolls in like a pale version of night
all around you, till your thin path
between land and sea
seems impossibly secure.
Far off, the foghorns moan faintly
like the ghosts of distant cattle;
and the shushing of the waves
is from the ghost of the sea.
Everyone else has simply
ceased to exist.
You are a ghost
in the ghost of a landscape.
Your path stretches briefly
from fog into fog,
a grey-white sanctuary
of air and water,
the soft secure shelter
of the cold and the damp.

Bastard Bloody Stutter

ONE OF THE CHATTIER MEMBERS OF STAFF AT THE JOB CENTRE asked me which we prefer to call ourselves, stammerers or stutterers. I liked the way he used the plural, the idea that I might speak (if I *could* bloody well speak) for all of stammerer-and-stuttererdom.

Stammer or stutter? The fact is, it makes no bloody difference: they're both as bloody hard to say.

But for what it's worth, the term I personally favour is bastard bloody stutter because I'm quite good at saying 'B's and the two of them together give me a good run-up at the difficult bit.

'R's on the other hand are nearly as difficult for me as 'S'es, so it's just as much trouble getting a single or return ticket at the station; so roll on maximum automation and self-service I say (or *would* say if I bloody well could), because though I know it would be easier I still can't bring myself to ask for a bastard bloody single to bastard bloody Central.

A Cup Of Tea In Stormsville

When I found out that Rory Storm, the Merseybeat singer-guitarist, had a terrible stutter too, I looked up a few articles about him. They say that the members of his band, The Hurricanes, wouldn't let him tell jokes or go to the bar himself when it was his round because it took too long. He was fine when he was singing, of course, but not when he was just talking. Also, and this is not to do with his stutter, his real name was Alan Caldwell, but he was so keen on his stage name that he adopted it by deed poll, and he called his house Stormsville.

Apparently when he had visitors he'd sometimes sing his bits of the conversation. So, for example, when he was offering them tea, he'd even sing the words, 'Would you like a cup of tea?' because it was so much easier than trying to just say them.

Seeing as how in my case I not only can't talk, but also can't sing either, none of this actually gets me very far. But still, I find it oddly comforting, almost as if I were sitting there now, enjoying a cup of tea in Stormsville.

The Good News, The Bad News, & The Therapeutic Chorus

BEARER OF THE GOOD NEWS & THE BAD NEWS:
Yes, I think you're doing quite well at this level. Now, if we can build up your confidence a little more at this level, & then we'll see about moving you up a little.
Now, the intensive course is booked up, I'm afraid, & the next one won't be for a while now: it's the cuts, really, it can't be helped.
Now if we could hear you again at this level, because you seemed to be doing quite well. It's mainly a matter of building up confidence.

THERAPEUTIC CHORUS (to the tune of *America*):
Bubbubbubbuilding up confidence.
Bubbubbubbuilding up confidence.
Bubbubbubbuilding up confidence.
Bubbubbubbuilding up con-fi-dence!

The Life And Soul

I don't do talk or how-do-you-do.
If it needs a word, I'll leave it to you.
I tend to be hushed as the morning dew,
or a man of the Illuminati.
If someone's talking, it won't be me:
I keep my words under lock and key,
but secretly I want to be
the life and soul of the party.

The life and soul,
and a slice of the whole,
with the give and the grab
of the gift of the gab.
But my words won't dance
so I daren't take a chance
and I keep what's there:
the empty air.

I need my silence as my prop.
It won't be me who nips to the shop.
If it's a talking part, I'd rather swap.
I don't do loud or hearty.
That's me in the corner, acting dumb.
If you want my opinion, the word is mum,
but all along, I long to become
the life and soul of the party.

Two Hours To Go

Two hours to go
before my first speech therapy group session,
and I find a sudden extra thing
to worry about.
Suppose I'm uncomfortable with everybody
and I turn out like the worst of stutterees:
being smoothly patronizing
as if anyone who stutters must be stupid;
or fidgeting impatiently;
embarrassedly shifting my eyes all over the place;
incompetently attempting
to finish people's sentences for them;
urging people to slow down;
urging people to hurry up;
and behaving generally
like a crypto-fascist arsehole?

Jonah

Jonah writes fantasies
where the hero
as thin as himself
is pitted against a
harsh authoritarian world
but always wins through
and wins also
the beautiful girl.
In the harsher ordinary world
he twitches, blinks
and dithers endlessly
even though the question
was only whether
he is coming down the pub;
and the minutes pass
while he debates out loud with himself
erming and stuttering the while,
discovering every possible reason
why it is simply impossible,
and sometimes I just want to tell him
to pull himself together
but other times I'm frightened
by how much he is like how I was
and yet other times I'm frightened even more
by how much he is like
how I still am.
His stutter has grown a body
around him, has swallowed
him whole long ago,
and now he is still living there,
inside the stutter,
able to travel only those oceans
the stutter swims,
able to call out only the brief distant word
from the bowels of the stutter
on those occasions
it breaches for air.

Twitch

In these speech exercises
odd things are starting to happen.
All G had to do
was talk about hippies,
but the way he started talking
like an unfunny comedy Nazi
suddenly had me wondering
what the hell he was hiding.
All H had to do
was discuss 'Things I Value'
when he point-blank refused
on grounds that it was idiotic,
as if practically every other exercise
we'd done wasn't.
Now all I have to do
is role-play as a rent arrears officer,
but somehow
I have turned into a rent arrears officer
who leans over backwards as he talks
and is now developing
a twitch beneath first one eye
and then both of them.
What a mess we all are.
What a mess we all are.
What a mess we all are.

Intensive Speech Therapy Course, Day 9

At the cafeteria in Binn's
we're gathering en masse
to take a break from our street assignments
though not from the technique,
and after nine days of talking
it's getting tough
to think of things to say.

They should make a stupid film about us
and call it *Carry On Thinking Of Things To Say*,
for somehow we manage it,
and the gems of our conversation
sparkle gently
in their uncut brilliance.

'Arrre youuu goinggg doo havvve
zummm zhugar innn your govveee?'
asks Colin in a moment of inspiration.
'Yezzz,' I reply with the rapier-like wit
of someone who has never
handled a rapier in his life;
'I vhinggg I *willl* havvve
zummm zhugar innn my govveee.'

The bad news
(for it would be foolish to deny
that there *is* some bad news)
is that we sound
like a slow motion replay
of a convention of Afrikaner idiots.

But the good news
(Mary, our head therapist,
should be pleased to notice)
is that it is a convention
of *fluent* Afrikaner idiots.

The 'Before' Film

There I am, freshly turned 23,
just me talking to the camera
against the blackness of the studio backdrop –
I remember when I was doing this,
how happy I was
they'd got me on a good day –
and look at me talking:
talking so fast –
I'm a boxer in the ring,
tense, jerking, bobbing;
I'm ducking and dodging,
sweat glistening in the spotlights.
I can see myself grimacing
at each invisible jab –
and I want to tell myself
to stop closing my eyes
or I won't see the knock-out punch
I'm sure must be coming.

Another 'Before' Film

Philomela doesn't stutter much;
but when she does, you know it.
Of all these stutters I now know so well,
I think it's the only one that,
when I first heard it,
made me feel something like shock:
a showstopper of a stutter,
the incredibly rapid repetition
of the same single syllable
over and over, in a high
but ever-changing pitch.
Even now, watching her 'before' film
from two weeks ago,
my heart goes out to her
as she struggles and struggles
just to talk. But at the same time,
I am suddenly hearing in the soundtrack
something different,
something strangely beautiful
in those same sharp
and ever-modulating notes,
as, by the purest of accidents,
she sings like a bird.

Five Minutes / It Was Never Like This

A microphone,
a bar-roomful of people
and it's as easy as this.
For five minutes
I am possessed
by myself.
For five minutes
the words I wrote
come out
of my mouth.
For five minutes
I can talk
and the words
don't stick.
Five minutes,
every sentence
flowing
just as I intend.
Five minutes, and shit!
Not only
do people listen;
they even
clap
at the end.

***

It was never like this
before having a stage.
It was never like this
for a stuttering age.
It was never like this
in school year four.
It was never like this
till the open floor.
It was never like this
being made to read.
It was never like this
being third-degreed.
It was never like this
at the ticket booth.
It was never like this
anywhere in truth.

So I want one of these
and I want one like this,
and I'll speak with an ease
that'll flow like pure bliss.
Yes, a neat little stage
I can carry around
that when I need to speak
I'll set up on the ground
right next to each person
I need to address,
and no more will I garble
a stuttery mess,
for I'll stand there and speak
in most fluent oration,
then graciously smile
as I take my ovation.

Coming Down

    Come-down's coming.
Getting nervous at the station.
Got to name my destination
& my gut's feeling rotten.
    Come-down's coming.
I must have forgotten;
Thought I'd left it all behind
But though it seems so unkind
    Come-down's coming:
Here comes the real mean trivia
Returning from Oblivia
& this is what we find:
    Come-down's coming.
You look at me so blank,
I could do with a tranq.
I'm in a bit of a hole.
    Come-down's coming
And it's taking control:
My voice is paralysed
& all the exits are disguised.
    Come-down's coming.
Got to face all the faces
& those tough commonplaces.
I think I want to pass.
    Come-down's coming:
So leaden, so crass.

Avoidance Tactics

Why I Hate Doing Street Assignments With Other People From The Group

It's a gently sunny summer evening, and we're doing street assignments in Liscard Village. I'm doing mine with Gordon, who like me has been coming to the sessions for a while, and with Julia, a student speech therapist who's just joined us for this session. I hate doing street assignments with other people from the group. Unless I've got a task I genuinely need to do, then having a therapist or another group-member with me just emphasizes to me that I'm being a fraud, which is always guaranteed to make me self-conscious.

Anyway, we've agreed it's Gordon's turn first, at the off-licence. We walk straight past it. 'Why did we just walk straight past it?' I ask. Gordon says he thought I was doing my assignment first.

We turn around and walk back towards the offy. As we approach it again, I slow down to let Gordon in first. Gordon slows down. I slow down some more. We all slow down. I affect a serious limp, and Gordon finally goes in, and we follow.

Inside, Gordon looks at the sweets for a few seconds, then moves along the counter to where the assistant is standing, and promptly blocks. Julia and I are standing trying to look like normal people waiting while a friend buys something. We can't really start chatting in the background, because if I happen to stutter it'll just make Gordon more self-conscious; and besides, Julia is meant to be monitoring Gordon.

Gordon keeps on blocking: every few seconds he tries to start again, and makes a slight noise before going silent again.

The other shop assistant asks Julia and me if we want anything, and I say, 'No, thanks,' though afterwards I think maybe I should have bought something, just to take a bit of attention away from Gordon, and also to distract me so I don't succumb to the laughter that I can feel evilly creeping up on me.

Finally Gordon blurts out, 'A box of matches please,' not really using the technique, and the girl understands him, thank god.

We go outside and walk off. No one says anything for a few seconds. I say, 'That was atrocious,' then immediately wish I'd kept the thought to myself.

Julia asks Gordon what he thinks of how it went.

Gordon says that he blocked, but that he was fine once he got started.

Well, yes.

Afterwards, I clumsily but successfully ask for some tobacco at the Boot Inn, who don't have any, and for the time from a man who doesn't have a watch. It's just as well I don't need any tobacco or care what time it is.

Just One Sonetto (Sonetto Faceto)

Ah! Once I was a quiet sort of guy:
A stutter tends to make you go that way.
Tell jokes or chatter freely? No, not I.
My stillness was perfection on a tray.
But then I grew impatient with my hush,
So now I let my words into the light:
The chat-ups and the jokes; the clumsy rush –
There's just no doubt: my social skills are shite.

If I could just shut up, I might look deep;
But sometimes people *do* catch what I say,
And that stupid, static silence wasn't cheap,
So I reckon how I am is how I'll stay:
The clumsiest, facetiousest of blokes,
Still stumbling from the blunders to the jokes.

The Utter Glamour
(For Jean Sprackland)

I have been thinking.
I have been thinking very hard
in magnificent isolation
about my stutter
and I have come to a conclusion,
and I have concluded
that at least three-quarters of the trouble
with the stutter
is just bad marketing.

What the stutter has got
is the wrong image.
Most people perceive it
as something clumsy, ugly, time-wasting
and also generally a bit pathetic;
and those people
just need to be helped,
helped to realize
how wrong they are;
and the way to do this
is to market the stutter
as a luxury item.

People (especially pretty women)
need to realize that the stutter
(especially my stutter)
is quite classy; that not only
Emperor Claudius but also
Albert Einstein, George VI
and James Bond all had stutters,
James Bond's stutter in particular
having a certain elegant *je ne sais quoi*
as displayed by David Niven
in the first movie of *Casino Royale*.

Yes, I can see it all now:
people (especially clever and really pretty women)
only need to realize the true attractiveness of the stutter:
starting say with the block stutter,
the poise of my lips,
the sensual closing of my eyes,

the delicate hesitation,
the suspense of the pause;
yes, women only need to realize
that women like a man who keeps them,
like a man who keeps them,
like a man who keeps them
waiting on his words
– for who knows what depths
lie beyond that silence? –
and the man with a stutter
is a man of mystery,
and women's hearts flutter
as they give up all resistance.

And I haven't even got
to the repeat stutter yet:
the leisure to treasure
each rough precious consonant,
to savour each syllable
over and over.
Ah yes! – people
(especially clever, gorgeous women)
only need to realize
the irresistible attraction,
the tonguing and tonguing
that might last forever;
the vigour of the stutter,
the masculine hammering
with its endless potential,
a jack-hammer stammer
with its unspoken promise
of paradise in the sack.

Yes, it's clear that people
(especially bright and fantastically gorgeous women
say a little under my own age)
need to be aware of these things,
helplessly, helplessly aware of them,
yes, so helplessly aware,
that at my first slight stutter
they can't help but find

they're getting moist already;
and it's clear that other people
(especially confident and hunky good-looking men
with flash cars and cushy overpaid jobs)
also need to be aware of these things,
need to be hopelessly aware
of the clattering inadequacy
of their own feeble fake speech impediments
as they try pathetically
to jump on the stammering bandwagon,
need to despair in jealousy and awe
at the overpowering allure of the real thing
which *I have* in abundance,
yes, abundance and triumph!

Ah, the stutter!
Ah, the stammer!
Ah, the utter,
utter glamour!

The Stutter Rides Off Into The Sunset (Unfortunately At Roughly The Same Speed As Myself)

These days mostly
my stutter's just a shadow of itself,
almost ghostly.
Though now and then
it will rise up and bite me, hard,
in the throat once again,
now mostly it
is just a thing that makes people think:
Oh, he stutters a bit.

But the year-on-year
the stutter had me on my own
still won't just disappear;
after all, any kid
who stuttered once, remembers,
even when they're long rid;
others stutter badly still,
and we echo each other,
and always will.

So even when I spout
my fluent words, and my fluent words
come nicely out,
I'm aware
of the lurking, silent stutter
that's always still there:
the repeat and the block
running through me, like Blackpool,
like Brighton,
through a stick of rock.

In Praise Of The Human Voice

(For all humans, but especially my speech therapists)

The human mouth can make the words
That speak out from the soul.
For stating complex concepts,
It's our most important hole.

I'm glad to have my human voice
Although it's got a stutter.
I'm glad I'm not a stick or stone
Whose silence is quite utter.

I feel my voice can help me
Each time I want to speak.
I'm glad that I can talk with words
And don't just honk or squeak.

From human mouths all round the world
Our human voice speaks out.
I'm glad I have a human mouth,
And not a beak or snout.

I'm glad to have my human voice
To say the things I feel.
My style would get quite cramped if I
Could only grunt or squeal.

I feel my voice can say things:
The things I want to say.
I don't think I'd think that, if I
Could only snort or neigh.

So many words in human mouths!
So common! So sublime!
They're using words to change the world
And just to pass the time.

I'm glad I have a human voice
And not that of a rabbit.
I learnt to talk, aged twenty-three,
And now it's quite a habit.

I feel my voice is useful.
If I'm lucky, you do too,
And we can say all kinds of things
Instead of Woof or Moo.

I feel my voice is useful.
I'm glad that I can speak.
I'm glad that we can talk with words
And not just honk or squeak.

The British Stammering Association

'It's a world that turns away again, before you've even met it.'

THE BRITISH STAMMERING ASSOCIATION IS THE UK'S NATIONAL CHARITY offering support, advice and information on all aspects of stammering. More than 700,000 adults and children in the UK are affected by stammering, and experience a world that, as in David Bateman's poem, often turns away from them before they've had a chance to meet. Far from being a mere mechanical speech production issue, stammering can become a severe communication disability.

Children who stammer can have problems with social interaction with others at school, becoming withdrawn and lacking confidence; they often experience bullying by their peers. In adults stammering can affect their personal and professional relationships and career choices (often leading them to accept jobs well below their capabilities). Stammering can also have a negative influence on a person's mental wellbeing and has in extreme cases led to suicidal thoughts and actions.

At the heart of our charity is our Information and Support Service. This includes a helpline and email answering service, a specialist education helpline, support groups and an online presence. In addition, we promote awareness of stammering, for example through our Employers Stammering Network, and support research, in furtherance of our vision of a society where everyone who stammers has as much chance of a full and rewarding life as everybody else.

Since 1978 well over a hundred thousand people have been helped with our expert knowledge of stammering and therapy options. We are a user-led charity which is mainly run by those who stammer.

For more information on the work of the British Stammering Association please visit www.stammering.org